MW01277389

AMERICA

JESS BRALLIER

AND SALLY CHABERT

JESS BRALLIER is the author of eight books including *The Hot Dog Cookbook* and *Lawyers and Other Reptiles*.

SALLY CHABERT has coauthored several books with her husband Jess.

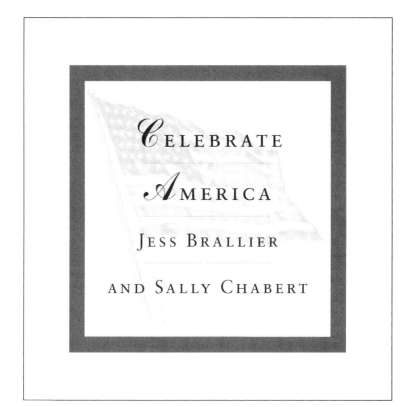

Celebrate America

America

Jess Brallier

and Sally Chabert

A Perigee Book

A Perigee Book
Published by The Berkley Publishing Group
200 Madison Avenue
New York, NY 10016

Book design by Joseph Perez
Cover design by Dale Fiorillo

The quote by John Updike that appears on p. ix is from *Summer,* edited by
Alice Gordon and Vincent Virga, and is used by permission of the author.

The quotes by George Plimpton that appear on pp. 81 and 107 are from *Fireworks,*
and are reprinted by permission of Russell & Volkening as agents of the author.
Copyright © 1984 by George Plimpton.

First edition: July 1995

Published simultaneously in Canada.

Library of Congress Cataloging-in-Publication Data
Brallier, Jess M.
    Celebrate America / Jess Brallier and Sally Chabert. — 1st ed.
      p. cm.
    ISBN 0-399-51943-2 (alk. paper)
  1. Fourth of July—Miscellanea. 2. Fourth of July celebrations—
Miscellanea.   I. Chabert, Sally.   II. Title.
    F286.A1253   1995
    394.2'684—dc20   94-24985
                                    CIP

Printed in the United States of America.

10 9 8 7 6 5 4 3 2 1

This book is printed on acid-free paper.

To Pat and Bob

"The first of earthly blessings, independence."

—*Edward Gibbon*

ℐNTRODUCTION

"This most American of holidays serves to remind us,
if we care, that our founding fathers, wearing wigs and jabots
and lace-trimmed frock coats, met and debated in a fearful
sweat, and delicately and artfully stitched together our national
fabric amid the muggy, buggy heat of a Philadelphia summer
before air-conditioning and pesticides."

—*John Updike*

The Fourth of July is America's very best holiday. Its only purpose is to celebrate our country. And with lots of noise. In 1777, when the folks in Philadelphia simply started to party, by shooting rifles, enjoying spirits, lighting candles, and waving banners, a holiday was born.

The Fourth of July is the holiday every American *wants* to celebrate. It is not forced upon us by legislation or religious mandate. You just *do it*.

The Fourth of July is pure festivity, no mourning, no frightening middle-aged renderings of sacrificial religious figures, no sad marches, sour trumpets, or depressing processions. Instead, it's the one holiday on which you're *supposed* to be rowdy and have fun. Go ahead, *Yell* out the window! *Scream* on the street. *Bang* your pots and pans! Celebrate America!

The Fourth of July is a summer holiday, an outdoors bash— perfect for noise! It *feels* healthy. No school! No homework! No harvest!

On the Fourth of July, hot dogs are not only expected, they're even encouraged—the food police take a holiday. Go ahead, have another dog. And some more potato salad. The baked beans are great. And hey, how about that apple pie?

Go ahead, feel good. Be proud. Act cocky. Enjoy it. On this day, a new idea of infinite scope was let loose in the world. Those who proclaimed their freedom, and made it good by force of arms, fought not only for political independence, but also for the kind of freedom that comes into the front yards and kitchens of ordinary people. Individuals were to no longer be dictated to. Families were to no longer be hungry. And the minds and hearts of generations to come were to no longer be restrained by a tightly ordered monarchy.

Stop for just one day to celebrate every principle and dream for which America stands, to which every other inhabitant of the world strives. Celebrate the brilliant articulation of these ideas and ideals "in terms so plain and firm as to command their assent" (Thomas Jefferson). And celebrate, with pride, John Hancock's bravery on July 4, 1776, when he signed the Declaration of Independence: "With a firm reliance on the protection of Divine Providence, we mutually pledge to each other our Lives, our Fortunes, and our sacred Honor."

Abraham Lincoln once said of July 4th celebrations, "We go from these meetings in better humor with ourselves, we feel more attached, the one to the other, and firmly bound to the country we inhabit."

We hope you'll feel much the same, after having read *Celebrate America*.

Jess Brallier and Sally Chabert
The Bancroft House (c. 1787)
Reading, Massachusetts
July 4, 1994

THE ENDURING CELEBRATION

*T*he idea of celebrating the birthday of our nation began in Philadelphia, where on July 4, 1777—according to John Adams in a letter to his daughter—bells rang out across the city, bonfires blazed against the night sky, and candles burned late into the evening.

For Adams, the day began at one o'clock, when the sailors of the warships—which were dressed with flags and lined up in the river—were ordered aloft on "the tops, yards and shrouds, making a striking appearance . . . of companies of men drawn up in order in the air."

Adams then boarded the *Delaware* with John Hancock, President of the Continental Congress, where they were greeted by a salute of thirteen guns, in succession, from each ship. At the City Tavern, a dinner with music furnished by "a band of Hessians taken prisoner at Trenton" was served at three o'clock. Between the many boastful toasts to a nation which had not yet won its freedom—a company of soldiers assembled outside the tavern fired continual volleys in celebration of the country's first birthday. After dinner, the many soldiers stationed in or about Philadelphia paraded about the city.

Adams took a walk that evening and "was surprised to find the whole city lighting up their candles at the windows. I walked most of the evening and I think it was the most splendid illumination I ever saw; a few surly houses were dark, but the lights were very universal. Considering the lateness of the design and the suddenness of the execution I was amazed at the universal joy and alacrity that was discovered and the brilliancy and splendor of every part of this joyful exhibition." The celebrating patriots broke the windows in the houses which were not illuminated, assuming the inhabitants were Loyalists.

The celebration of the Fourth of July gradually spread throughout the country and into the new states and territories as they were admitted to the Union or as they were created, until the day was a holiday in every state and territory.

"Within our own borders we possess
all the means of sustenance, defense, and
commerce; at the same time, these advantages
are so distributed among the different
states of this continent as if nature
has in view to proclaim to us—be united
among yourselves, and you will want
nothing from the rest of the world."

*—Samuel Adams, in a speech
on American Independence,
delivered on July 4, 1776*

Why July 4th?

On July 4, 1776, the Declaration of Independence was adopted by the Second Continental Congress and signed by Charles Thomson, secretary of the Congress, and John Hancock, its presiding officers.

"There, I guess King George will be able to read that."

—John Hancock, on the exaggerated size of his signature, as he placed it on the celebrated document

"We must all hang together or assuredly we shall all hang separately."

—Benjamin Franklin, to Hancock at the initial July 4th signing

Almost a month later, on August 2, other members signed a parchment copy, though their names were withheld from the public to prevent their arrest and hanging as traitors.

"This day will be the most memorable epoch
in the history of America. I am apt to believe that it will
be celebrated by succeeding generations as
the great anniversary festival. It ought to be
commemorated as the day of deliverance, by
solemn acts of devotion to God Almighty. It ought
to be solemnized with pomp and parade, with
shows, games, sports, guns, bells, bonfires, and
illustrations, from one end of this continent to the other,
from this time forward forevermore."

—*John Adams, in a letter to
his wife, Abigail*

★

Declaration of Independence, July 4, 1776

(its first 182 words)

"When, in the course of human events, it becomes necessary for one people to dissolve the political bands which have connected them with another, and to assume, among the powers of the earth, the separate and equal station to which the laws of nature and of nature's God entitle them, a decent respect to the opinions of mankind requires that they should declare the causes which impel them to the separation.

"We hold these truths to be self-evident, that all men are created equal, that they are endowed by their Creator with certain unalienable rights, that among these are life, liberty, and the pursuit of happiness. That, to secure these rights, governments are instituted among men, deriving their just powers from the consent of the governed. That, whenever any form of government becomes destructive of these ends, it is the right of the people to alter or to abolish it, and to institute new government, laying its foundation on such principles, and organizing its powers in such form, as to them shall seem most likely to effect their safety and happiness. . . ."

THE CRITICAL COMMENTARY

"A more impudent, false, and atrocious Proclamation
was never fabricated by the hands of man."

—Ambrose Serle,
secretary to Lord Howe

"If the American Revolution had produced nothing but the
Declaration of Independence, it would have been worthwhile."

—Samuel Eliot Morison

"I was in the State House Yard when the
Declaration of Independence was read. There were
very few respectable people present."

—Charles Biddle, on the first
public reading of the document,
on July 8, 1776, in Philadelphia

★

"This was the object of the Declaration of Independence. Not to find out new principles, or new arguments, never before thought of, not merely to say things which had never been said before; but to place before mankind the common sense of the subject, in terms so plain and firm as to command their assent, and to justify ourselves in the independent stand we are compelled to take."

—*Thomas Jefferson*

AUTHOR! AUTHOR!

"Jefferson had a happy talent for composition."

—John Adams

*A*lthough the Continental Congress appointed five delegates to write the Declaration, it was essentially written by the pen of one man, Thomas Jefferson. (There were, of course, as there are in any political or publishing process, several rounds of editing, including the deletion of Jefferson's attack on the slave trade.) In 1782, John Adams offered his version of how the author came to be Jefferson:

Jefferson proposed to me to make the draught.
I said, "I will not."
"You should do it!"
"Oh! no."
"Why will you not? You ought to do it."
"I will not."
"Why?"
"Reasons enough."

"What can be your reasons?"

"Reason first—You are a Virginian, and a Virginian ought to appear at the head of this business. Reason second—I am obnoxious, suspected, and unpopular. You are very much otherwise. Reason third—You can write ten times better than I can."

Whether the choice of Jefferson was ingenious, luck, or divine intervention, it was surely perfect. Jefferson was a brilliant writer. Historians note that if the irrepressible Ben Franklin had written the Declaration, it would have been peppered with jokes; and if it had been John Adams, the writing would have been contentious and turgid; but with Jefferson, the new nation nobly declared its independence with sentiment and clarity.

Jefferson took great pride in the Declaration and its impact upon history's course of events. In fact, the epitaph he wrote for himself identifies him as the author of the Declaration of Independence, and *not* as a former President.

"Jefferson's Declaration of Independence is a practical
document for the use of practical men. It is not a
thesis for philosophers, but a whip for tyrants; it is not a
theory of government, but a program of action."

—*Woodrow Wilson*

"REMEMBER THE LADIES . . . ."

On March 31, 1776, before John Adams and the other delegates to the Second Continental Congress began finalizing any documents, his wife, Abigail, wrote to remind him that the female half of the population must not be forgotten:

> In the new Code of Laws which I suppose it will be necessary for you to make I desire you would remember the Ladies, and be more generous and favourable to them than your ancestors. Do not put such unlimited power into the hands of the Husbands. Remember all men would be tyrants if they could. If particular care and attention is not paid to the Ladies we are determined to foment a Rebellion, and will not hold ourselves bound by any Laws in which we have no voice, or Representation.
>
> That your Sex are Naturally Tyrannical is a Truth so thoroughly established as to admit of no dispute, but such of you as wish to be happy willingly give up the harsh title of Master for the more tender and endearing one of Friend.

Why then, not put it out of the power of the vicious and the Lawless to use us with cruelty and indignity with impunity? Men of Sense in all Ages abhor those customs which treat us only as the vassals of your Sex. Regard us then as Beings placed by Providence under your protection and in imitation of the Supreme Being make use of that power only for our happiness.

—from Abigail Adams, in
Braintree, Massachusetts, to
her husband, John Adams,
in Philadelphia, Pennsylvania,
on March 31, 1776

Birthday Trivia!

America's birthday is also celebrated in Denmark, Norway, Sweden, and Britain. In Denmark, where people listen to songs and speeches about the friendship between the United States and Denmark, the celebration is known as *Rebildfest*.

Delaware's delegation to the Continental Congress put at risk a unanimous endorsement of the Declaration. Delaware delegate George Read was adamantly opposed to the Declaration (many still harbored an affinity for Great Britain and others feared for their careers and the fate of their families), while fellow Delawarians Thomas McKean and Caesar Rodney favored its adoption. And it appeared that Rodney, who was suffering from terminal cancer, would arrive in Philadelphia a day too late to break the Delaware delegation's deadlock. However, the insistent Rodney rode all night through darkness, lightning, and thunder to arrive just in time to cast his affirmative vote, without which the declaration would not have been unanimous. Phew!

16

In the 1890s, it was customary to celebrate July 4th with two parades: in the morning, a burlesque "Horribles" parade of men and boys dressed in fantastic costumes and making noise with all sorts of devices, and in the afternoon a second parade featuring military veterans and members of various local organizations.

Thomas Jefferson played cards to relax while he was writing the Declaration of Independence.

The names of the signers of the Declaration of Independence were withheld from the public for more than six months because, if independence were not achieved, their treasonable act would, by law, result in their deaths.

Until Henry Ford invented the automobile, the Fourth of July was traditionally the most miserable day of the year for horses, tormented by all the noise and by the boys and girls who threw firecrackers at them.

THE REPUBLIC
BY
HENRY WADSWORTH LONGFELLOW

Thou, too, sail on, O Ship of State!
Sail on, O Union, strong and great!
Humanity, with all its fears,
With all the hopes of future years,
Is hanging breathless on thy fate!
We know what Master laid thy keel,
What Workmen wrought thy ribs of steel,
Who made each mast, and sail, and rope,
What anvils rang, what hammers beat,
In what a forge and what a heat
Were forged the anchors of thy hope!
Fear not each sudden sound and shock,—
'Tis of the wave and not the rock;
'Tis but the flapping of the sail,
And not a rent made by the gale!
In spite of rock, and tempest's roar,
In spite of false lights on the shore,

Sail on, nor fear to breast the sea!
Our hearts, our hopes are all with thee,
Our hearts, our hopes, our prayers, our tears,
Our faith, triumphant o'er our fears,
Are all with thee,—are all with thee!

SIGNERS OF THE
DECLARATION OF INDEPENDENCE

"While General Howe with a Large Armament
is advancing towards New York our Congress resolved
to Declare the United Colonies Free and Independent
States. A declaration for this Purpose, I expect
will this day pass Congress. . . . It is gone so far
that we must now be a free Independent State or
a Conquered Country."

*—Abraham Clark, member of the
Continental Congress from New
Jersey, in a letter to Elias Dayton,
Philadelphia, July 4, 1776*

Throughout 1775 and early 1776, most Americans—including delegates of the Continental Congress (except for the odd radical troublemaker like Sam Adams)—simply saw themselves as being in active and well-justified rebellion against their rightful king. They hoped that the king would install a new government and institute new policies, but still remain their sovereign. Three-quarters of the colonists were descended from English families; their Bible, their prayer books, and their schoolbooks were written in English; and the history they learned and the heroes, saints, and martyrs they revered, were English.

So it was an especially inspiring yet solemn occasion when upon the document's very last line, these patriots, by their signatures, pledged—

And for the support of this Declaration, with a firm reliance on the protection of Divine Providence, we mutually pledge to each other our Lives, our Fortunes, and our sacred Honor.

THE SIGNERS — MINI-FACTS

All fifty-six of those who signed the Declaration eventually suffered, to some extent, from physical hardships, loss of loved ones, financial failure, and damage to—and in some instances, complete destruction of—their families.

21

All but eight of the signers were native-born.

Of the foreign-born, two were from England, one from Wales, two from Scotland, and three from Ireland.

They lived to an average age of sixty-six years.

Three lived into their nineties!

They were prolific producers of children, averaging six per father.

Two were bachelors.

About one-third of the signers were wiped out financially.

Robert Morris, an extremely wealthy patriot, known as "Financier of the Revolution," lost his fortune in land speculation after the Revolutionary War. With debts of three million dollars, he was sent to debtor's prison in 1798. Although he was penniless, the prison charged him rent for what Morris called his "hotel with the grated door." His cell included a writing desk, bedstead, settee, chairs, and mirrors, and his visitors were as varied and distinguished as Alexander Hamilton and George Washington. Five years after completing his three-and-a-half-year sentence, Morris died in poverty and obscurity.

Thomas McKean of Pennsylvania once wrote to John Adams, "I have had my full share of the anxieties, cares, and troubles of the present war. For some time, I was obliged to act as president of the Delaware state and as chief justice of this; General Howe had just landed at the head of the Elk River when I undertook to discharge these two important trusts. The consequence was to be hunted like a fox by the enemy, and envied by those who ought to have been my friends. I was compelled to remove my family five times in a few months and at last, find them in a little log house on the banks of the Susquehanna, more than a hundred miles from this place; but safety was not to be found there, for they were soon obliged to remove again, on account of the incursions of the Indians."

THE SIGNERS

NAME	AGE AT DECLARATION	COLONY	PROFESSION
John Adams	40	Massachusetts	lawyer
Samuel Adams	53	Massachusetts	businessman
Josiah Bartlett	46	New Hampshire	physician
Carter Braxton	39	Virginia	planter
Charles Carroll	38	Maryland	lawyer-planter
Samuel Chase	35	Maryland	lawyer
Abraham Clark	50	New Jersey	politician
George Clymer	37	Pennsylvania	banker
William Ellery	48	Rhode Island	lawyer
William Floyd	41	New York	farmer
Benjamin Franklin	70	Pennsylvania	publisher
Elbridge Gerry	31	Massachusetts	merchant
Button Gwinnett	41	Georgia	merchant
Lyman Hall	52	Georgia	physician
John Hancock	39	Massachusetts	merchant
Benjamin Harrison	50	Virginia	planter
John Hart	65	New Jersey	farmer
Joseph Hewes	46	North Carolina	merchant
Thomas Heyward, Jr.	29	South Carolina	lawyer
William Hooper	34	North Carolina	lawyer
Stephin Hopkins	69	Rhode Island	merchant

NAME	AGE AT DECLARATION	COLONY	PROFESSION
Francis Hopkinson	38	New Jersey	lawyer
Samuel Huntington	45	Connecticut	lawyer
Thomas Jefferson	33	Virginia	lawyer-planter
Francis Lightfoot Lee	41	Virginia	planter
Richard Henry Lee	44	Virginia	planter
Francis Lewis	63	New York	merchant
Philip Livingston	60	New York	merchant
Thomas Lynch, Jr.	26	South Carolina	lawyer-planter
Thomas McKean	42	Delaware	lawyer
Arthur Middleton	34	South Carolina	lawyer-planter
Lewis Morris	50	New York	landowner
Robert Morris	42	Pennsylvania	financier
John Morton	52	Pennsylvania	farmer
Thomas Nelson	37	Virginia	planter-merchant
William Paca	35	Maryland	lawyer
Robert Treat Paine	45	Massachusetts	lawyer
John Penn	36	North Carolina	lawyer
George Read	42	Delaware	lawyer
Caesar Rodney	47	Delaware	planter
George Ross	46	Pennsylvania	lawyer
Benjamin Rush	30	Pennsylvania	physician

NAME	AGE AT DECLARATION	COLONY	PROFESSION
Edward Rutledge	26	South Carolina	lawyer-planter
Roger Sherman	55	Connecticut	lawyer-merchant
James Smith	57	Pennsylvania	lawyer
Richard Stockton	45	New Jersey	lawyer
Thomas Stone	33	Maryland	lawyer
George Taylor	60	Pennsylvania	iron-maker
Matthew Thornton	62	New Hampshire	physician
George Walton	35	Georgia	lawyer
William Whipple	46	New Hampshire	merchant
William Williams	45	Connecticut	merchant
James Wilson	33	Pennsylvania	lawyer
John Witherspoon	53	New Jersey	clergyman
Oliver Wolcott	49	Connecticut	politician-soldier
George Wythe	50	Virginia	lawyer

When in late June 1994, a survey was conducted as to the general public's favorite signer's name, the clear winner was Button Gwinnett, and the distant runner-up was Caesar Rodney.

> "Yesterday the greatest question was decided,
> which ever was debated in America, and a greater
> perhaps never was nor will be decided among men. A
> resolution was passed without one dissenting colony
> 'that these United Colonies are, and of right ought
> to be, free and independent states.'"
>
> —*John Adams, in a letter to
> Abigail Adams*

★

CHILDREN OF THE FOUNDERS

Countless thousands of heirs of the fifty-six signers of the Declaration of Independence are scattered throughout the country. One of the best known is retired attorney and professor Archibald Cox, a sixth-generation descendent of Connecticut's Roger Sherman. As the Watergate special prosecutor, Cox insisted that a President, like any citizen, is accountable under the law. Cox believed the Watergate drama was a profound affirmation of the faith that the Declaration of Independence places in ordinary citizens. For Cox, "the most moving scene" occurred when Watergate grand jurors— "a fair cross section of men and women, black and white"—were polled one at a time by Judge John J. Sirica about whether they wished to subpoena the taped conversations of President Nixon. "I wondered whether they would stand firm: Each one did. Now, suppose Roger Sherman had walked into that courtroom at that time. Would he not have been both exceedingly proud and comforted?"

"You observe that republics can exist and that people under that form of government can be happier than any other; that the republic created by the Declaration of Independence will continue to the end of time is my fervent prayer. That protracted existence, however, will depend on the morality, sobriety and industry of the people. . . ."

—*Charles Carroll, the last surviving signer of the Declaration, on July 4, 1828*

THE NATION'S HOROSCOPE
(SORT OF!)

In her 1975 masterpiece, *The True Horoscope of the United States*, Helen M. Boyd notes that "any astrological map for July 4, 1776, would of necessity be weak because of the lack of major aspects between the Sun (government) and Moon (people) plus the further evidence that neither of the Lights formed any aspect at all with Pluto. According to mundane astrology, when the Sun and Moon are opposite or square Pluto, respectively, the very heart of the people is affected. Pluto denotes the termination of alliances, breaking of contracts, and the like ('Planet of crises, it acts with dramatic decisiveness, leaving the status quo irrevocably altered, if not shattered.'—Cyril Fagan).

"But," Ms. Boyd further notes, "no such crisis took place on July 4th. Rather was the greater part of the day devoted to arguments and controversy. It is just this indifferent correspondence between actual fact and planetary forecast that has given many astrologers cause for concern. . . . In my opinion, [we have] valid, documented proof that *JULY 6, 1775 is the TRUE birthday for the United States of America.*"

THE LIBERTY BELL

What we know as The Liberty Bell was first cast, in 1751, in celebration of Pennsylvania's fiftieth birthday *as a British province* (its manufacture has nothing to do with the struggle for liberty or the American Revolution which occurred over twenty years later).

When the now famous bell was first rung, it cracked. So it was hauled off, melted down, and recast. But when this second bell was then rung, it sounded awful. So it was again melted down and recast, just in time *to ring in King George III's celebrated accession* to the throne in 1761.

Finally, turning from its British ways, the bell was rung to announce a reading of the Declaration of Independence on July 8, 1776. In 1828, Philadelphia tried to unload the bell as scrap, but had no takers. So they kept ringing it on various occasions until 1825, when it cracked again—permanently.

Then, at last, in the 1830s, sixty years after the Revolution, the name "Liberty Bell" was finally coined for the old bell—*by antislavery activists, and in reference to the liberty of African-Americans.* That's why it's called the Liberty Bell.

Anyway, the bell is now enclosed and protected, sitting next to Philadelphia's Independence Hall, probably awaiting the glorious return of the British Empire.

If you're curious, as of July, 1994, here's what is inscribed on the Liberty Bell.

[front and center]

Pass and Stow
[that's for John Pass and John Stow,
the guys who made the bell]

Philadelphia
1753

[and along the top of the bell, two lines]

"Proclaim liberty throughout all the Land unto all the inhabitants thereof." Lev. 25, 10

By order of The Assembly for the Province of Pennsylvania for the State House in Philadelphia

FROM DISTANT SHORES

The major immigrant groups of the mid-1800s were the Irish and Germans. Their impact on the Fourth of July was soon apparent.

In 1848, Charleston (South Carolina) celebrated July 4 with a parade, at the end of which an oration in German was featured, while in Indianapolis, the Declaration of Independence was read in both English and German.

And just four years later, in 1852, the New York City Fourth of July parade participants included—the Shamrock Benevolent Society, the Erin Paternal Benevolent Society of Brooklyn, the Hibernian Universal Benevolent Society of New York, the Roman Catholic Total Abstinence Society, the Irish American Society, and the Hibernian Benevolent Burial Society.

"It was not George III but Parliament who attempted to tax America. The most that can be alleged against the King is that he stood by Parliament in their quarrel with the American people. The Americans demanded

35

independence of Parliament, not separation from
the Crown. They were ready to acknowledge
George III as their King provided they were allowed
to govern themselves."

—*1776, the British Story of
the American Revolution*

Other nations also celebrate America and the spirit of
freedom represented by July 4th:

Zambia
(Heroes Day). On July 4th, the country celebrates a
national holiday in which political rallies stress solidarity.

Canada
(American Visitors' Party). Welcomes American tourists
on their special day. The celebration features a really big
birthday cake and a Tourist-of-the-Year Award!

The Caribbean Community

(Caribbean Day). This is a public holiday celebrating the Treaty of Chaguaramas, signed on July 4, 1973, by the prime ministers of Barbados, Guyana, Jamaica, Trinidad, and Tobago.

The Philippines

(Philippine-American Friendship Day). This public holiday features floral ceremonies at the American battle monuments and other observations honoring American freedom.

Italy

(Garibaldi Day). The Italians celebrate the July 4, 1807, birthday of Giuseppe Garibaldi, the most forceful figure in the nineteenth-century unification of Italy.

★

SELECTIONS FROM THE PRIVATE JOURNALS OF THE DECLARATION OF INDEPENDENCE

July 2, 1776:
My birthday! Tom Jefferson, my creator, today submitted me to the Second Continental Congress. Phew, is it ever hot here in Williamsburg!

July 4, 1776:
I'm exhausted! I've really been worked over. These guys changed a third of me—and between you and me, I don't think Tom's too pleased about it. But so be it, they've at last settled on the words I am now. Charlie Thomson signed me, as did John Hancock. Boy, that guy, what a signature!—I swear he tickled me halfway up my back!

August 2, 1776
Another exhausting day. Fifty more delegates signed me. Some of these guys are really nervous. Once they've signed me, you know, they'll hang for treason if captured by those damn Brits.

January 7, 1790

Wow, what a wild four years this has been. When the British invaded Philadelphia, they put me in a trunk and everybody who had signed me had to run for their lives. Me too. I've been to York, down in Pennsylvania. Over to Annapolis, in Maryland, and then to New Jersey, to the city of Trenton. Hey, that's a lot of traveling for a chunk of paper like me. Then when the good guys finally won and that Washington fellow was elected President, he decided I ought to be here, in New York City, the nation's capital, to take up residence in the office of his secretary of state. And just guess who that is—my creator! Tom Jefferson! Really! Isn't that something? Back together after four of the wildest years the world's ever seen.

August 20, 1814

I'm in some minister's home in Leesburg— that's in Virginia—hiding from those Brits again. Geez! You know, I'd just like to get settled at some point, like most any other decent document. You see, after they hauled me up to New York City, they changed the capital to Philadelphia, so they hauled me down to there, then they decided this Washington place, in the District of Columbia, would make for a better capital, so then they dragged me down here. And just when I thought my moving days were over, here come the British again, aiming to burn me. And they still are. That's why I'm hiding here in the dark, in Leesburg. Boring!

February 10, 1821   I think that maybe, just maybe, this time I've settled. After those damn Brits were finally chased out of Washington, I returned from Virginia. But what a mess it was here! I swear half the buildings had been burned. So they've moved me time and time again. But now they've had me here at the Department of State for over a year. Let's keep our fingers crossed. One problem, though, I'm all rolled up. I'll get stiff and sore, I just know it.

December 31, 1841   What a year this was! The new secretary of state, Daniel Webster, figured I should be on view—damn right!—and so had me unrolled—aahhh! . . . that felt sooo good . . . after twenty years—and then mounted and displayed. That's right—I'm the featured display in the Department of State's newest undertaking, the Patent Office.

August 2, 1875   This isn't good. I don't feel well. I've been hanging here for thirty-four years. I've gone yellow. It's that window over there, the one directly across from me. I'm fading in its light. Doesn't anybody care? Don't people notice? Are these government workers idiots?

July 4, 1876   I'm back! In Philadelphia! For the big Centennial Exposition. Has it really been one hundred years since all those brave men put pen to me? But oh no, my yellowed and faded presentation would shame them all. Some of those great names can't even be read anymore.

I can't help it. I just can't hold the inks, year in and year out, against the air and sun. At this rate, I'll never make it to the Bicentennial. Oh my, what an amazing thought. Two hundred years. It burns the imagination.

December 3, 1877   Holy smokes, that was close! They moved me, just this year, from that awful Patent Office to here, at the Department of State library. And then what do you know, the Patent Office burned just months after my move. I'd have been nothing but ashes!

January 5, 1894   They've got to do something. I feel awful and look worse. Been hanging here at the State Department library for seventeen years. There's just got to be a better way.

January 1, 1900   1900! Amazing! I wonder if the boys of 1776 in Philadelphia ever thought we'd be around this long, and be this big! Anyway, since 1894, I've been tucked between two plates of glass and locked in here, a steel safe in the State, War, and Navy Building. It's restful, and at least, for the most part, my health's not worsening.

December 31, 1921   Hey, what a year this has been. They put me in the damndest thing—something called a Model T—and moved me over to the Library of Congress. It's a much nicer section of town, but really, these senators and representatives fall far short of the great men who wrote all over me. You would really think that with all the people in this country now, you'd be able to find a few boys with brighter bulbs than they have here! Anyway, the really great news is that they brought all these fancy, highbrow document experts in from all over the country to examine me. And they decided to put me back up on display. This time, however, the lighting is perfect, real soothing, none of this harsh, burning stuff. I love it.

December 26, 1941 I'm on the run again. But this time it's not from the Brits, but from the Germans and Japanese. The people in charge expect that plans are afoot to bomb buildings throughout Washington. So they've stuck me in a bronze container, provided me with a Secret Service guard, and I'm traveling on a Pullman to Fort Knox, Kentucky. Evidently I'll be put in some underground vault within the Bullion Depository. So much attention for little old me, just a brittle piece of paper!

October 1, 1944 This World War II mess isn't over yet, but I guess the enemy's on the run and it's safe to bring me back to the Library of Congress. The quarters here are really something! I'm sealed in insulating glass with the air expelled, and they've put special paper next to my back to suck up moisture and help me endure any possible temperature change. And here too, the lighting is perfect. But best of all, they've got these special guards from the Army, Navy, and Marines watching over me. I can't imagine better accommodations.

December 14, 1952 Wow, they did it. Even *better* accommodations. Yesterday they moved me to this new Archives Building. And what a move it was! I was in an army armored personnel carrier escorted by tanks, an army band, and troops with machine guns. Then they put me in here, in this bulletproof helium-filled display case. Better yet, and get a load of this, with the push of a button, my whole display goes through the floor, down twenty-two feet, and into a fifty-five-ton vault built of steel and reinforced concrete. I think I'm safe now.

October 2, 1994 What a great day! I just found out that I'm going to be a published author. Really. Seems that two folks up in New England are putting together a book entitled *Celebrate America,* and they want to include some of *my* writings. Boy, wouldn't old Tom be proud of me! I could just cry with joy.

TOP TEN JULY FOURTH TUNES

10. "The Star-Spangled Banner"
 9. "Yankee Doodle"
 8. "America"
 7. "You're a Grand Old Flag"
 6. "Chester"
 5. "America the Beautiful"
 4. "The World Turned Upside Down"*
 3. "Birthday Song"
 2. "The Battle Hymn of the Republic"
 1. "The Red, White, and Blue"

* In 1781, upon the final British surrender at Yorktown, a fife-and-drum corps played the British soldiers out to the field of surrender, tooting this sprightly, appropriately ironic, little tune.

LETTERS OF REGRET

In 1826, ceremonies were being planned throughout the country to celebrate the fiftieth anniversary of Independence Day. The citizens of Quincy, Massachusetts, invited the ailing ninety-one-year-old John Adams to join in their festivities. The mayor of Washington, D.C., sent a similar invitation to the indisposed eighty-three-year-old Thomas Jefferson. In sending their regrets, both ex-presidents heralded the significance of the day.

JOHN ADAMS TO THE CITIZENS OF QUINCY

Quincy, June 7, 1826

Sir,

Your letter of the 3rd Instant, written on behalf of the Committee of Arrangements, for the approaching celebration of our National Independence; inviting me to dine, on the fourth of July next, with the Citizens of Quincy, at the Town Hall, has been received with the kindest emotions.

The very respectful language with which the wishes of my Fellow Townsmen have been conveyed to me, by your Committee, and the terms of affectionate regard toward me, individually demand my grateful thanks, which you will please to accept and to communicate to your Colleagues of the Committee.

The present feeble state of my health will not permit me to indulge the hope of participating with more than by my best wishes in the joys and festivities and the solemn services of that day, on which will be complete the fiftieth year from its birth, the independence of the United States: A memorable epoch in the annals of the human race, destined, in future history, to form the BRIGHTEST OR THE BLACKEST PAGE according to the use or the abuse of these political institutions by which they shall, in time to come, be shaped by the human mind.

I pray you, sir, to tender, in my behalf to our fellow-citizens, my cordial thanks for their affectionate good wishes, and to be assured that I am very truly and affectionately yours and their friend and fellow-townsman,

J. Adams

THOMAS JEFFERSON TO THE MAYOR OF WASHINGTON

Monticello, June 24, 1826

Respected Sir,

The kind invitation I received from you, on the part of the citizens of the city of Washington, to be present with them at their celebration of the fiftieth anniversary of American Independence, as one of the surviving signers of an instrument pregnant with our town, and the fate of the world, is most flattering to myself, and heightened by the honorable accompaniment proposed for the comfort of such a journey. It adds sensibly to the sufferings of sickness, to be deprived by it of a personal participation in the rejoicing of that day. . . . I should, indeed, with peculiar delight, have met and exchanged there congratulations personally with the small band, the remnant of that host of worthies, who joined with us on that day, in the bold and doubtful election we were to make for our country, between submission or the sword; and to have enjoyed with them the consolatory fact, that our fellow-citizens, after half a century of experi- ence and prosperity, continue to approve the choice we made. May it be to the world, what I believe it will be (to some parts sooner, to others later, but finally to all), the signal of arousing men to burst the chains under which monkish ignorance and superstition had persuaded them to bind themselves, and to resume the blessings and security of self-government. . . . All eyes are opened, or opening, to the rights of man. The general spread of the light of science has already laid open to every view the palpable truth, that the mass of mankind had not been born with saddles on their backs, nor a favored few booted and spurred, ready to ride them legitimately, by the grace of God. These are grounds of hope for others. For ourselves, let the annual return of this day forever refresh our recollections of these rights, and an undiminished devotion to them. . . .

With my regret that ill health forbids me the gratifica- tion of an acceptance, be pleased to receive for yourself, and those for whom you write, the assurance of my highest respect and friendly attachment.

Th: Jefferson

BIRTHDAY TRIVIA!

July 4th, a legal holiday in all states and United States territories overseas, is one of the few holidays that have not been moved to the nearest Friday or Monday.

The word "patriotism" comes from the Latin *patria,* which means "homeland" or "fatherland."

The Declaration of Independence was first . . .
reproduced on July 6,
read to the public in Philadelphia at noon on July 8 (where, according to one observer, there were few "respectable" people),
read in New York "in a clear voice" by order of General George Washington, July 9, and
read in Boston, accompanied by church chimes and the firing of cannons, on July 18.

Actually, in Williamsburg, the Colonial capital of Virginia, Independence Day is celebrated on July 25, for news of the adoption of the Declaration at Philadelphia did not reach there in 1776 until three weeks later.

The Statue of Liberty is a 151-foot (including the torch) woman with a 4-1/2-foot nose and 3-foot mouth. In her left hand, she holds a book upon which is written "July 4, 1776," and on her base is inscribed the following.

"Give me your tired, your poor,
your huddled masses yearning to breathe free,
the wretched refuse of your teeming shore,
send these, the homeless, tempest-tossed, to me:
I lift my lamp beside the golden door."

—*Emma Lazarus, author of
the inscription on the Statue
of Liberty*

★

Uncle Sam

With his red, white, and blue suit, top hat, pointy white beard, and the same initials as the United States, Uncle Sam is the illustrator or cartoonist's favorite symbol for the United States government. Face it: Compared to the flag or the bald eagle, it's just got to be a lot easier to work temperament and personality into some undefined old guy dressed in a goofy clown outfit.

But why Uncle Sam and not Aunt Mildred or Grandpa Ralph? The most widely accepted explanation is that during the War of 1812 a New York meat packer, Sam Wilson, who supplied the American Army with meat, stamped his barrels with "U.S." for "United States."

As the story goes, a visitor to Wilson's factory asked what the initials "U.S." stood for, and a worker jokingly replied, "Why, for Uncle Sam Wilson." Soon, in the mysterious way that these things work, American soldiers began to call their meat "Uncle Sam's meat." Then the story evolves a step further as the soldiers soon started to call themselves "Uncle Sam's Army"; and it was just a matter of another misplaced syllable here or there and the soldiers claimed that they "worked for Uncle Sam."

And suddenly Uncle Sam equals the United States government.

Uncle Sam's bright costume first began to appear in its current form in the 1830s, the very time, coincidentally, when a popular clown wore a similar outfit. Uncle Sam's beard first appeared in the 1860s and 1870s, when, coincidentally, beards were fashionable, especially in the White House (starting with Lincoln in 1860). Uncle Sam's popularity really hit full stride during World War I, when James Montgomery Flagg drew the famous "I Want YOU" recruiting poster.

CREED

BY
EDGAR A. GUEST

Lord, let me not in service lag,
Let me be worthy of our flag;
Let me remember, when I'm tried,
The sons heroic who have died
In freedom's name, and in my way
Teach me to be as brave as they.

In all I am, in all I do,
Unto our flag I would be true;
For God and country let me stand.
Unstained of soul and clean of hand,
Teach me to serve and guard and love
The Starry Flag which flies above.

THE AMERICAN FLAG

No other device—be it the eagle, the Liberty Bell, or Uncle Sam—evokes the feelings the flag does. Symbols are a shorthand method of telling a complicated story, and our flag immediately calls to mind the struggle of the thirteen original colonies united in the common cause of freedom.

> "When I think of the flag, I see alternate strips of parchment upon which are written the rights of liberty and justice, and stripes of blood to vindicate those rights, and then, in the corner, a prediction of the blue serene into which every nation may swim which stands for these great things."
>
> —*Woodrow Wilson*

THE SOMEWHAT OBSCURE AND UNCERTAIN HISTORY
OF THE AMERICAN FLAG BEGAN . . .

. . . in October, 1775, when Congress created the first naval force and set down rules for the creation of a flag. The result, variously called Congress Colors, the Grand Union Flag, or the First Navy Ensign, was a flag of thirteen alternating red and white stripes, with a field of blue bearing the crosses of St. George and St. Andrews. This flag is believed to be the one raised by Lt. John Paul Jones aboard the Hopkins's flagship, *Alfred,* on the Delaware River at Philadelphia on December 3, 1775. The first land raising of the Grand Union Flag occurred at Prospect Hill in Somerville, Massachusetts, on January 1, 1776, during the siege of Boston. On June 14, 1777, Congress adopted what became known as the Stars and Stripes, a flag of thirteen red and white stripes, with a blue field bearing thirteen stars, one for each state.

"Beautiful as a flower to those who love it,
terrible as a meteor to those who hate it,
it is the symbol of the power and the glory,
and the honor, of . . . Americans."

—*Senator George Frisbie Hoar,
on the flag (1878)*

THE TRADITION THAT BETSY ROSS . . .

. . . designed the flag has been almost completely discredited. It has been suggested that Francis Hopkinson, a member of the Continental Navy Board form 1776 to 1778, was the father of the Stars and Stripes.

OUR FLAG WAS STILL THERE

The flag that Francis Scott Key saw "by the dawn's early light" was hard to miss—forty-two by thirty feet. It had fifteen stripes instead of thirteen, and each one was two feet wide. It cost $405.90, required more than four hundred yards of cloth, and weighed more than two hundred pounds.

Major Armistead, commander of Fort McHenry during the War of 1812, hoped the flag would be "so large that the British will have no difficulty in seeing it at a distance." They didn't. Even after an all-night bombardment of the fort, which guarded the Baltimore harbor, they could see that "our flag was still there."

THE COLORS

In 1782, when the colors of the flag were made part of the Great Seal of the United States, the Department of State explained the colors and their meanings: *Red* stands for hardiness and courage; *white* is the symbol of purity and innocence; and *blue* is the color of vigilance, perseverance, and justice.

THE PLEDGE OF ALLEGIANCE

I pledge allegiance to the flag of the United States of America and to the Republic for which it stands, one nation under God, indivisible, with liberty and justice for all.

"Off with your hat as the flag goes by!
And let the heart have its say;
You're man enough for a tear in your eye
That you will not wipe away."

—*Henry Cuyler Bunner,*
"The Old Flag," 1888

63

THE STAR-SPANGLED BANNER
BY
FRANCIS SCOTT KEY

O say, can you see, by the dawn's early light,
What so proudly we hailed at the twilight's last gleaming?
Whose broad stripes and bright stars, through the perilous
    fight,
O'er the ramparts we watched were so gallantly streaming!
And the rocket's red glare, the bombs bursting in air,
Gave proof through the night that our flag was still there;
O! say, does that star-spangled banner yet wave
O'er the land of the free, and the home of the brave?

On that shore dimly seen through the mists of the deep,
Where the foe's haughty host in dread silence reposes,
What is that which the breeze, o'er the towering steep,
As it fitfully blows, now conceals, now discloses?
Now it catches the gleam of the morning's first beam
In full glory reflected now shines on the stream;
'Tis the star-spangled banner; O long may it wave
O'er the land of the free, and the home of the brave!

And where is that band who so valiantly swore
That the havoc of war and the battle's confusion
A home and a country should leave us no more?
Their blood has washed out their foul footsteps' pollution.
No refugee could save the hireling and slave
From the terror of flight, or the gloom of the grave;
And the star-spangled banner in triumph doth wave
O'er the land of the free, and the home of the brave.

O! thus be it ever, when freemen shall stand
Between their loved homes and the war's desolation!
Blest with victory and peace, may the heav'n-rescued land
Praise the power that hath made and preserved us a nation.
Then conquer we must, when our cause it is just,
And this be our motto—"In God is our trust":
And the star-spangled banner in triumph shall wave
O'er the land of the free, and the home of the brave.

On This Day in History, July 4th . . .

1776, in Philadelphia, while the Continental Congress is debating whether to accept the Declaration of Independence, its author, Thomas Jefferson, slips out of the proceedings to do some shopping. He buys one thermometer and seven pairs of women's gloves.

1777, in Philadelphia, all ships of the little United States Navy now in Philadelphia line up in the Delaware River, and as President John Hancock and several other members of the Continental Congress board the warship *Delaware*, they are saluted with thirteen guns; later, all members of Congress convene for a one-year-old birthday party at which a Hessian army band captured at Trenton entertains.

1778, members of the Continental Congress gather to celebrate in Philadelphia's City Tavern—thirteen toasts and music are featured— while over at Brunswick Landing in New Jersey, the Continental Army is served double rations of rum and told by General Washington to "adorn your hats with green-bough and to make the best appearance possible," fire three rounds, and give three cheers, each time shouting, "Perpetual and undisturbed independence to the

United States of America," a big step up from the traditional "hip, hip, hurrah!," and in Paris, John Adams and Benjamin Franklin attend the first ever overseas celebration of America's independence.

1783, commencement ceremonies are held at the University of Pennsylvania, and George Washington is given the honorary degree of doctor of law; meanwhile Charleston, South Carolina, which wishes to join the rest of the nation's communities in ringing bells, can't—the British took all of the town's bells during the Revolution—and for the first time, Boston celebrates July 4th— "The joy of the day was announced by the ringing of bells and the discharge of cannon."

1788, at sunrise in Philadelphia, its windy streets and wharves alive with hundreds of flags and pennants, residents are greeted by the pealing of bells and the boom of cannons from the ship *Rising Sun;* then, just several hours later, a parade of five thousand heads down Third Street—it features twelve axmen in white frocks (representing pioneers), a company of dragoons, and John Nixon, the patriot who gave the Declaration of Independence its first public reading at the State House in Philadelphia on July 8, 1776.

1800, Daniel Webster, an eighteen-year-old Dartmouth student, gives his first Fourth of July oration.

1802, West Point opens.

1804, Joseph Fields, who is accompanying explorers William Clark and Meriwether Lewis up the Missouri River, is suddenly bit by a snake; later in the day Lewis and Clark name a stream near Atchison, Kansas, "Independence Creek," a name it still bears.

1817, Governor DeWitt Clinton of New York turns the first sod to launch the digging of the Erie Canal.

1818, Charles Carroll, a signer of the Declaration of Independence, turns the first sod for construction of the nation's first railroad, the Baltimore and Ohio. "I consider this among the most important acts of my life, second only to that of signing the Declaration of Independence, if, indeed, second to that," he says.

1820, the annual celebrations in Baltimore again feature Charles Carroll, a signer of the Declaration of Independence.

1824, in New Haven, Connecticut, the Reverend Leonard Bacon of Center Church, delivers a sermon on African colonization, the first in what was to be a long series of Fourth of July colonization sermons supporting the effort to establish a home for free blacks in Liberia, Africa.

1825, the ladies of Pittsfield, Massachusetts, in celebration of Independence Day, invite the town's gentlemen to an evening tea party at a shaded park near the village.

1827, the menfolk of Poplar Springs, Georgia, manage to drink one hundred toasts to the nation's birthday.

1829, the Springfield, Massachusetts Colonization Society meets at Dr. Osgood's to hear an address on colonization, pray, sing some hymns, and collect eighty-one dollars to assist the Liberian colonists.

1830, it's Sunday, so this year's annual celebration—which features sixty Revolutionary War veterans riding in a special thirty-six-foot-long carriage drawn by eight horses—is moved to the next day, July 5.

1831, President James Monroe dies in New York City, making him the third of the nation's first five Presidents (the others being Thomas Jefferson and John Adams) to die on July 4th. Bells toll across the country as the nation mourns one of its last Revolutionary War heroes; and although he was impoverished due to the burdens of public service, plans for Madison's funeral procession promise that it will be the grandest the city of New York has ever seen.

1833, in Elyria, Ohio, four hundred citizens gather to hear a debate between Immediate Abolitionists and advocates of the American Colonization Society.

1834, the New York Anti-Slavery Society meets in the morning to hold integrated July 4th exercises in the Chatham Street Chapel but are disrupted by hecklers. (When they meet again on July seventh and their efforts are again interrupted by a white mob, a week of rioting follows—New York City's worst riots up to that time.)

1835, the USS *Constitution*, "Old Ironsides," pride of the United States Navy, stops by New York harbor and fires a salute from its many mighty cannons.

1837, in Troy, Wisconsin, an early settler reports in on their July 4th celebration, "There are only three of us in town and one gun, but we fired the gun."

1839, in Newburgh, New York, this year's bash boasts eight Revolutionary War veterans, the youngest—now age seventy-four—fought as a fifteen-year-old in the Battle of Yorktown, and the others are in or near their nineties.

1847, in Indianapolis, Indiana, a Revolutionary War soldier is introduced, and the holiday crowd is told to look carefully, for "this might be the last hero of the struggle for Independence" they would ever see.

1850, the cornerstone of the Washington Monument in the nation's capital is laid (after which President Zachary Taylor will rush back to the White House, drink some milk, eat a bowl of ripe cherries, get stomach cramps, and die five days later from food poisoning).

1851, Daniel Webster, secretary of state, gives his last Fourth of July oration, at the cornerstone-laying ceremonies for the expansion of the Capitol Building.

1855, Walt Whitman publishes, at his own expense, the volume of poems *Leaves of Grass* (it will soon be severely criticized for its "glorification" of sex).

1858, Cleveland, Ohio, invites a ninety-eight-year-old Revolutionary War veteran to join this year's festivities.

1860, New Yorkers enjoy the day at the sideshow exhibits over at Barnum's American Museum or visit Adam's California Menagerie (featuring "THE GREAT LIVING SEA LION, SINGING BEARS, CLIMBING BEARS, DANCING BEARS, VAULTING BEARS, BEARS THAT TURN SUMMERSETS!"), while others watch a parade of 7,000 soldiers march past City Hall.

1863, in the midst of the Civil War, the city of Vicksburg, Mississippi —the South's last major post on the Mississippi River—surrenders to the Union forces and President Lincoln notes, "the father of Waters again goes unvexed to the sea." On this same day, a battle in Gettysburg, Pennsylvania, comes to a devastating close for the South. Most Northerners jump to the conclusion that because these two great victories on one day are a clear indicator of divine favor, the war will be over by this time next year.

1864, at 10 A.M., a party of freedmen take over Jefferson Davis's empty plantation home in Mississippi (as president of the Confederacy, he and his family are living in Richmond) for the day, enjoying songs, food, and thirteen toasts! Meanwhile, those who had assumed last year that the war would be over by now are terribly disappointed.

1865, just months after General Lee's surrender at Appomattox, the North celebrates the Fourth with more enthusiasm than ever before—General Grant himself presents New York's governor with the battle flags of two hundred New York regiments; the cornerstone is being laid for the Soldier's Monument in Gettysburg; and every village and city is filled with bands, floats, dances, marches, and more!

1866, in a great conflagration ignited by the careless use of fireworks, Portland, Maine, burns to the ground.

1875, the mayor of Cincinnati bans the shooting of firecrackers and pistols in the street but his instructions are ignored, even by the police, who take "a general holiday and allow the boys to have full swing."

1876, at the country's Centennial Exposition in Philadelphia, Alexander Graham Bell introduces the telephone.

1883, the first Wild West Show, starring Buffalo Bill Cody, is held in North Platte, Nebraska.

1884, France presents the Statue of Liberty to the United States.

1895, "America the Beautiful," a poem by Katherine Lee Bates, a Wellesley College professor, is published in the *Congregationalist*.

1888, on the battlefield at Gettysburg, a great meeting of former soldiers of both the Union and Confederate armies is held.

1898, in the midst of the Spanish-American War, Admiral Sampson cables from Cuba, where his troops have destroyed the Spanish squadron without the loss of a single ship. Noted Admiral Sampson, "The fleet under my command offers the nation as a Fourth of July present the whole of Cervera's fleet."

1903, President Theodore Roosevelt inaugurates the new Pacific cable via Hawaii by sending a message to the Philippines; and in Pecos, Texas, the first rodeo with prizes is held.

1909, as part of the annual Bristol, Rhode Island, celebration, Professor Felix Porter's announced balloon ascension and parachute drop comes to an embarrassing conclusion when his balloon leaves the ground without him.

1918, with so many American soldiers stationed on British soil, or fighting side-by-side with English forces on the European continent, July 4th is celebrated for the first time in England.

1919, the greatest parade ever to march down New York's Fifth Avenue is mounted in celebration of the nation's victorious efforts in World War I.

YOUR JULY FOURTH BASH — WHY?

"Picnics, excursions, lawn-parties, and village gatherings, with open-air programs and plays, are now increasingly popular on the Fourth of July, and to be commended . . . . *The patriotic American mother* is anxious to celebrate Independence Day in such a manner as will impress her children with a sense of the freedom and independence which are their birthright. It devolves upon her to stimulate and encourage the patriotism of the younger members of the family by bringing to their minds as impressively yet as gayly as possible the significance of the anniversary, and *this she can do by an artistic decoration of the home with the national colors, and by a menu and table ornamentation that will be viewed with delight and remembered ever after with joy."*

—*The Delineator,* 1914. (Founded in 1875 as a fashion publication; *The Delineator* soon evolved into a magazine that developed recipes and cooking techniques while editorializing on such relevant issues of the day as child care and woman's suffrage.)

JULY 4TH BIRTHDAYS

In honor of all the great (and not so great) folks born on the Fourth of July, match the quote with the July 4th birthday boy (or girl).

1) Nathaniel Hawthorne (1804)
2) Stephen Collins Foster (1926)
3) Calvin Coolidge (1872)
4) Louis "Satchmo" Armstrong (1900)
5) Leona Helmsley (1920)
6) Ann Landers (1918)
7) Abigail Van Buren (1918)
8) Neil Simon (1927)

A) "I'm obsessed with winning, with discipline, with achieving. That's what this country's all about, that's what New York is all about—fighting for everything: a cab in the rain, a table in a restaurant at lunch time."

B) "Rose-colored glasses are never made in bifocals. Nobody wants to read the small print in dreams."

C) "Out!"

D) "That player has a God-given killer instinct."

9) George Steinbrenner (1930)

10) Geraldo Rivera (1943)

11) Pam Shriver (1962)

12) Al Davis (1929)

E) "What other dungeon is so dark as one's own heart! What jailer so inexorable as one's self!"

F) "If you want a place in the sun, you've got to put up with a few blisters."

G) "If you gotta ask what jazz is, you'll never know."

H) "I think the American public wants a solemn ass as President and I think I'll go along with them."

I) "I was mobbed by viewers (young girls, mostly) wherever I went; like a rock star with a hit record, I would stop traffic, turn heads, and start a crowd."

J) "The physical labor actors have to do wouldn't tax an embryo."

K) "O Susanna!"

L) "Only the little people pay taxes!"

ANSWERS: 1—E, 2—K, 3—H, 4—G, 5—L, 6—B, 7—F, 8—J, 9—A, 10—I, 11—C, 12—D.

★

FOURTH OF JULY THROUGHOUT THE LAND

"I always thought July Fourth was the best day of
the year. . . . When you got up in the morning someone
would almost surely say that it was going to be a 'true
Fourth of July scorcher.' . . . And of course, the best
thing about the day was the anticipation of fireworks."

—*George Plimpton*

Centreville, Maryland
(American Redneck Day). This is a celebration of the work-hard,
play-hard, independent spirit of the rural working class.

Main Street, Willimantic, Connecticut
(Boom Box Parade). No *real* bands allowed! Marching band music is
played by boom boxes along the parade route. "Anyone can march—
but you've gotta have a radio! Anyone can enter a float—but you've
gotta have a radio! Anyone can watch—but you've gotta have a radio!"

Sponsored by The Naturist Society Oshkosh, Wisconsin
(Nude Recreation Week). This week promotes acceptance of the body and understanding of the nude recreation movement as a natural solution to many problems of modern living.

Oatman, Arizona
(Oatman Sidewalk Egg Frying Contest). High noon! Only solar heat allowed! Thirty-minute time limit! Old West gunfights! Wild burros roam the streets!

Lee Richardson Zoo, Garden City, Kansas
(Zoobalee). Turtle races! The Annual Animal Mimic Contest (animal sounds)! And even more!

Bristol, Rhode Island
(Bristol Civic, Military and Firemen's Parade). Since 1785! The nation's oldest Fourth of July parade!

Lake Waramaug, New Preston, Connecticut
(Frog Jump Jamboree). Kids under sixteen are welcome to enter their favorite frogs. Old-fashioned fun. No entry fee!

Rotary Riverview Park, Sheboygan, Wisconsin
(The Great Cardboard Boat Regatta). Lots of prizes, including the Titanic Award—for the most spectacular sinking!

Mt. Rushmore National Memorial, South Dakota
(Mount Rushmore Fourth of July Celebration). Features "dramatic" sculpture-lighting program!

Fort Lauderdale, Florida
(Sandblast). A sand-sculpture competition on Fort Lauderdale beach for both amateurs and professionals. Plus fireworks!

Gatlinburg, Tennessee
(Gatlinburg's July 4th Midnight Parade, 12:01 A.M). Always the very first July 4th parade in the nation. Thousands of lights! Weird floats!

Ithaca, New York
(National Country Music Day). For those who love real American music—country music!—on a real American day. Lots of picking!

Burton, Ohio
(Muzzle Loading Shoot). Real Americans in costume demonstrate target and novelty black-powder shooting. Lots of noise!

Creston, Iowa

(Ten Thousand Crestonians). July 4th celebration. Approximate attendance: 10,000.

Fishkill, New York

(The Annual Reading of the Declaration of Independence). For over ninety consecutive years, residents of Fishkill have gathered outside Village Hall to hear the Declaration of Independence read aloud. The tradition was almost broken in the late 1940s when Mary Bogardus, a local businesswoman, and Sarah Taylor, who would later become the village's mayor, went to the hall in a driving rainstorm only to find the door to the premises locked. Just to keep the tradition intact, they stood under an umbrella on the steps and read the Declaration with no one but Mrs. Taylor's little dog as an audience.

Rock River, Rockford, Illinois

(Anything that Floats Rock River Raft Race). Rafts compete for speed and creativity. Wet! Lots of sinking!

Lovington, New Mexico

(World's Greatest Lizard Race). Children's lizards! Features a racecourse with a sixteen-foot ramp.

Biwabik, Minnesota

(Calithumpian Parade). A funny parade—clowns, clowns, clowns, and more clowns! Featuring a town with a population of over 1,490!

Lititz Spring Park, Pennsylvania

(Fairyland of Candles). During the winter, for over one hundred years, residents of Lititz have made thousands of tallow candles in old-fashioned tin molds, which on the evening of the Fourth are then lit and placed throughout the park, with many floating on the park's waters.

Shelburne, Vermont

(Shelburne Museum's Old-Time Farm Day and Grand Old Fourth). Animals! Cow-milking! Butter-churning!

Hannibal, Missouri

(Tom Sawyer Fence-Painting Day). Features prize-winning contests and activities based on the famous episode from Mark Twain's *Tom Sawyer.*

THERE'LL ALWAYS BE A BRISTOL (RHODE ISLAND)

Bristol, Rhode Island, which has been celebrating July 4th for as long as is possible—since 1777—is unlikely ever to top the events of its 1854 celebration. That year, several houses were set on fire by firecrackers and by the wadding from fired guns. According to the local newspaper, *The Bristol Phoenix,*

> "A portion of the wadding of one of the guns lodged upon the roof of the Baptist church and set it on fire. . . . A lad named Morris, about twelve years of age, ascended by the lightning rod and attempted to extinguish the flames by scraping dust upon them with his feet, but finding it of no avail, he began to spit upon them. Still flames increased until he had the presence of mind to unbutton his pants and play his own engine so effactually that he entirely extinguished the fire. A large crowd . . . greeted the lad with loud huzzahs."

★

"BILL OF FARE FOR AN INDEPENDENCE DAY PICNIC OF FORTY PERSONS"

BY

MRS. BEETON

*(a writer of cookery books
who was the Julia Child of the
nineteenth-century kitchen)*

"A joint of cold roast beef, a joint of cold boiled beef, two ribs of lamb, two shoulders of lamb, four roast fowls, two roast ducks, one ham, one tongue, two veal-and-ham pies, two pigeon pies, six medium-sized lobsters, one piece of collared calf's head, eighteen lettuces, six baskets of salad, six cucumbers.

"Stewed fruit well sweetened, and put into glass bottles well corked; three or four dozen plain pastry biscuits to eat with the stewed fruit, two dozen fruit turnovers, four dozen cheesecakes, two cold Cabinet plum-puddings (this must be good), a few baskets of fresh fruit, three dozen plain biscuits, a piece of cheese, six pounds of butter (this, of course, includes the butter for tea), four quarter loaves of household bread, three dozen rolls, six loaves of tin bread (for tea), two plain plum cakes, two pound cakes, two sponge cakes, a tin of mixed biscuits, half a pound of tea. Coffee is not suitable for a picnic, being difficult to make."

TOP DOZEN
NEAT IDEAS FOR YOUR JULY 4TH BASH

1. Make invitations of blue ink on white paper, rolled and tucked into giant firecrackers (paper tubes covered with red paper, with a string "fuse" in one end), then ask kids (they love this!) to toss the firecracker/invitations at all the neighborhood homes!

2. Do the actual invitation in rhyme. Like this:

   > Roses are red,
   > Violets are blue,
   > It's at the home of Fred,
   > on the Fourth that you're due.

   Or far better yet, include one of the simple poems from this book.

3. Ask your guests to wear only red, white, and/or blue. Be sure to take plenty of photos—all that red, white, and blue looks great and makes for a different (yet equally perfect) invitation for next year's bash (just send a print as a postcard invitation—write right on the back!).

4. Three words: hydrangeas, hydrangeas, hydrangeas.

5. Line your driveway or front walk with flags (the little parade-style ones, stick them right in the ground)—and lots of them! Looks great and every kid can go home with one.

6. Bubbles! Kids love bubbles! Great for the outdoors! Perfect for summer! Keeps the little tykes busy. Entertaining for all ages (be sure to videotape the grown-ups hogging all the fun!). Stock a hearty supply of wands and bubble solution.

7. Customized T-shirts for your guests! Kids and adult sizes! Red, white, and blue! "I survived July 4th at the Simpsons" or "July 4, 1995, with the Nelsons" or better yet, be creative!

8. Face-painting! Load up on red, white, and blue. A surefire winner with kids! And even the stuffier adults—after a couple of hours in the sun—will get into the red-nosed/blue-eyed/white-cheeked spirit of the country's most glorious day.

9. Set your buffet table with seasonal flowers in the national colors (geraniums, roses, poppies, alyssum, larkspurs, corn-flowers) or—in *abundance*—with whatever is currently blooming.

10. A Corn Shucking Contest! Hey, why not?—eliminates the worst part of your food preparation. Inexpensive! Perfect for all ages! Sober or not! Get messy!

11. Decorate, decorate, decorate! In red, white, and blue! Flags, stars, liberty bells, paper fireworks, firecrackers, streamers, crepe paper, tissue paper, ribbons, stickers, and printed paper!

12. Games! Lots of games! All-American games! Like Pin the Tail on Uncle Sam, Musical Chairs (patriotic tunes only!), George Washington's White Horse Race (run on all fours), Dunking for Apples, Treasure Hunt, and Ring Toss.

First, the Table

Don't approach this issue lightly. After all, the buffet table is your centerpiece, whether it's a family heirloom in your dining room, a picnic table under the apple tree, or a Ping-Pong table in the barn.

Cover the table with a white cloth, stretch tricolored streamers down its middle, and top with a centerpiece of red and white flowers—and American flags!—in a container of blue. Around the overhang of the tablecloth, arrange a zigzag of streamers by folding and pinning the points to the tablecloth.

Wrap silverware in napkins and insert into "firecrackers" (same as suggested invitations, above; i.e., empty paper tubes covered with red paper and featuring a string "fuse"). Stack these firecrackers at one end of the table (they look menacing and clearly project the message "You better enjoy this food!").

FOURTH OF JULY SERVINGS

For Something Traditional

Deviled Eggs
Radishes
Homemade Pickles
Cold Fried Chicken
Hot Dogs
Hamburgers
Gingerbread
Sugar Cookies
Lemonade

For Something Southern

Smoked Pork Shoulder
Southern Baked Beans
Crispy Coleslaw
Hard Rolls
Peach Ice Cream

94

For Something from Ebony Magazine

Zesty Lime Cornish Hens

Watermelon Fruit Boat

Black-Eyed Pea Salad

Vegetable Kabobs

Pineapple Tea

Old-Fashioned Apple Pie

For Something Different

Backyard-on-the-Grill Lamb Shanks

Grill-Top Tomatoes

Hot Relish

Parsley Rice

French Bread

Ice Tea

Blueberry Pie

95

The Ultimate Fourth of July Serving — A Day of Dogs

Fabulous Frankfurter Fact #1

In 1976, the grand eastern seaboard city of Philadelphia celebrated the American Bicentennial with the unveiling of a five-foot-long, 1,776-ounce hot dog.

Fabulous Frankfurter Fact #2

Americans eat 1 *billion* hot dogs in July.

Fabulous Frankfurter Fact #3

If hot dogs are slashed, they will curl into fun shapes as they heat! Stand them up! Top them off with parsley—they'll look like July 4th trees! Decorate them with red, white, and blue miniature marshmallows—they'll look like patriotic octopus!

Breakfast
Uncle Sam's Frankfurter Frittata

Lunch
Rev. Townsend's Split Pea and Hot Dog Soup

Ye Olde Supreme Wiener Salad

Jimmy's Louisiana Black Dogs

Dinner
Crown Roast of Dogs

IF YOU BORE OF BEER, GO PATRIOTIC!

Stars and Stripes

1/3 Grenadine
1/3 Heavy Sweet Cream
1/3 Blue Curacao

Now, here's the cool trick—*pour carefully, very carefully, and in above order* into pousse-café glasses, so that each ingredient floats on the preceding one. This is a beauty, often bringing tears to veterans of the Big One.

Liberty Cocktail

3/4 oz. Rum
1-1/2 oz. Apple Brandy
1/4 teaspoon Sugar Syrup

Stir with ice and strain into cocktail glass. Serve while whistling "Yankee Doodle."

Betsy Ross Cocktail

1-1/2 oz. Brandy
1-1/2 oz. Port
1 dash Triple Sec

Stir with cracked ice, strain into cocktail glass, and top with one of those little American flags mounted on a toothpick (perfect opportunity to rediscover the bizarre joys of your local party goods store).

Boom Boom Punch

2 quarts Rum
1 quart Orange Juice
1 fifth Sweet Vermouth
1 bottle chilled Champagne
2 bananas, sliced (optional)

Perfect for the fireworks show. Pour the first three ingredients over a large block of ice in a punch bowl. Now add champagne. For purposes of health and decoration, float the slices of banana.

★

The Best Lemonade Ever
(non-alcoholic)

3 lemons, scrubbed
granulated sugar, as desired
1 quart boiling water
chipped ice

optional:
    currant, strawberry, or raspberry juice
    banana, strawberries, raspberries, or pitted cherries

Chop off thin outer skin of the lemons and steep the peelings for 10 minutes in a little water. Cut 2 thin slices from the center of each lemon and set aside. Juice all of the remaining lemons. Add sugar to the juice as desired, then add the boiling water and the strained water from steeped peel. Let stand until cool, then refrigerate until needed.

Serve with slice of lemon and chipped ice. A little currant, strawberry, or raspberry juice may be added. Slices of banana, strawberries cut in quarters, or raspberries or pitted cherries on cocktail skewers make great garnishes.

Makes 1 quart.

A FOURTH OF JULY ACROSTIC

Flutter of Flags and of streamers gay
Over the dusty and sunlit way.
Underneath in the crowded street
Rattle of drums and clatter of feet.
Trumpets and cannon, confusion and noise,
Here, there, and everywhere, crackers and boys.

Out in the darkness, when evening comes,
Flashing of rockets and wheels and bombs.

Joyous feasting, frolic and fun,
Under the trees when the snow is done.
Lanterns and laughter—enough, I say,
You shall tell me the name of the day!

—Anonymous

THE FOURTH AND
THOSE MARVELOUS FIREWORKS

"'What are fireworks like?' she had asked.
'They are like the Aurora Borealis,' said the King, 'only
much more natural. I prefer them to stars myself, as you
always know when they are going to appear. . . .'"

—*Oscar Wilde,*
The Remarkable Rocket

The somewhat obscure and uncertain history of fireworks must first begin with gunpowder, which supposedly begins in China. Maybe. You see, *what* country is not as certain as *who did what* is— in this case, *a cook goofing around*. In ancient times the components of gunpowder were also common kitchen ingredients: saltpeter (potassium nitrate, used as a salt substitute), sulfur as a flammable solid, and charcoal (from charred wood). It's easy to assume then that some cook at some point noticed that when this mixture was burned, it did so with style and force. Then when that cook goofed off even further, and jammed the mixture into a bamboo shoot stopped up at both ends, and took a match to that—it exploded! *Voilà!* Just the perfect thing—with a few modifications—for frightening off spirits, celebrating weddings, and eventually, the Fourth of July.

Fireworks were standard fare for the July 4th celebration as early as 1778. In 1805, Boston had its first Fourth of July fireworks, and being a city never to miss out on a political opportunity, it was determined that the sky show feature the emblazoned busts of Washington and Hamilton. By 1900, Fourth of July fireworks were a $10 million industry. Their use on the Fourth came about, largely, to supplant an even more dangerous tradition—the firing of guns to make noise. The growing popularity of firecrackers during the period after the Civil War, and the resulting decline in firearms-related injury, argued forcefully in favor of fireworks. The Fourth of July novice must also remember that during this period—between the Civil War and World War I—the firecrackers in use were mostly of the Chinese black-powder variety, rather than the more potent chlorate/aluminum photoflash variety.

As the Fourth approached, fireworks shops would open in every American city, offering favorites such as prismatic whirligigs, batteries of stars, volcanoes, Pharaoh's serpents eggs, yellow jackets, and incendiary devices of every imaginable variety. Adults and children crowded these establishments as they crowd toy shops before Christmas, buying hundreds of dollars' worth of fireworks and firecrackers.

Yet such fireworks caused the holiday to be filled not only with their awful noise, but also plenty of death and maiming. For example, at the Battle of Bunker Hill, 449 colonists were killed and wounded by the British, while on July 5, 1904, 4,169 Americans were killed and wounded by fireworks. A year later, the number of dead and wounded was up to 5,176. Every July 4th, Americans were dying at an alarming rate. The crisis become so serious in the early 1900s that the sensible citizenry began to demand a saner means of celebration. San Francisco, for example, which was still reeling from the terrible earthquake and fire of April 1906, banned the sale of fireworks in July of the same year. This was also the dawning of the so-called Progressive Era: social engineering through organized pressure groups, propaganda, and legislation to bring about such utopian reforms as the Temperance movement and its brainchild, Prohibition. Fireworks became an especially favorite target of a campaign that reached its zenith in the pages of the *Ladies' Home Journal* throughout the summer of 1911. Such demands soon lessened the carnage: The loss of life from fireworks throughout the nation fell from 466 to 215 in just six years.

★

"Fireworks provided a sort of equalizer,
especially for those kids who were not good at sports,
and were taken last on the pickup teams, and knew
they were doomed to spend most of the long summer
afternoons in the far reaches of right field when they
were not stepping up to the plate and striking out.
They too on the Fourth of July had the capacity to
create something just as satisfactory as a ball caught
up against the fence, or a base hit—and make a
big racket about it besides."

—*George Plimpton*

As of the mid-1990s, private, customized fireworks parties have become increasingly popular. For his son's wedding, Sheik Hazza bin Zayid, the sultan of Abu Dhabi, had Fireworks by Grucci create a sky-high celebration that included a tableaux-type camel race and a grand finale of the sultan's portrait in glittering lights. However, at a cost of between $4,000 and $300,000, these parties leave most of us Americans on the Fourth still holding nothing more than a sparkler.

DOUBLE CROSSWORD ENIGMA

My firsts are in flower, but not in tree;
My seconds, in soldier, but not in free;
My thirds are in sunrise, but not in day;
My fourths, in October, but not in May;
My fifths are in watchman, but not in gun;
My sixths are in earth, but not in sun;
My sevenths, in monastery, but not in bell;
My eighths, in confess, but not in tell;
My ninths are in junk, but not in shop;
My tenths are in prude, but not in fop;
My elevenths, in library, but not in book;
My twelfths are in yeast, but not in cook;
My wholes both delight Young America.

—Marie Townsend,
age 7 (1904)

JOKE TIME!

Ruby: Are you going to work tomorrow, Daddy?

Dad: Nah!—tomorrow's a holiday, nobody works on July Fourth.

Ruby: I know something that works—fireworks!

"JULY 5"
(AN EXCERPT FROM *BRITE AND FAIR*)
BY
HENRY A. SHUTE

Published in 1920, Brite and Fair *is a humorous book of fiction in the form of a diary, kept by a semiliterate adolescent boy with a bit of Huck Finn and a lot of Bart Simpson in him.*

July 5. brite and fair. i was so tired last nite that i coodent wright. i dident go to bed unitl nearly leven and i got up at 2 oh cloc. it was the best 4th i ever had. Pewt's cannon xploded the ferst time. we loded it to the muzle and put the muzle rite agenst the stone step of old Nat Weeks house. then we lit the fusee and run. i gess it is lucky we done it for there was a feerful bang and a big flash jest like when litening strikes a tree rite in front of your house and a big hunk of that cannon went rite through old Bill Greenleaf's parlor winder and took sash and all and gnocked a glass ship in a gloab that the glassblewers blowed into forty million peaces and gnocked a big hunk out of the marbel table top and sent things on the wahtnot all over the room.

Bill he come downstairs in his shert tale and hollered and swore so you cood hear fer eight miles eesy. me and Pewt and Beany hid behind Pewts fathers paint shop and lissened. Nat Weeks he come out and old printer Smith and old bill Morrill. Old Ike Shute dident./ i gess he dident dass to. we cood hear them talking it over and cood hear Bill holler and sware and Bills wife say mersy sakes aint this dredful. they thoght it must have been did by Flunk Ham and Chick Randall or the Warren boys, all big fellers to have sutch a big cannon. so me and Pewt and Beany clim over Fifields back fence and went down town throug Spring Street.

Beany se tfire to a bunch of fire crackers in his poket and birnt him so he can only sit down on one side. Fatty Melcher dtumped Pewt to hold a fire-cracker in his mouth an dlet it go off. it is enuf. all you have got to do is put the end betwen your teeth and lite the other end and shet your eys. it will go off and burst in the middle and all you will get is a few sparks that dont hurt mutch. but his one was a flusher and flaushed at the whitch was in Pewts mouth and a stream of sparks went rite down Pewt's gozzle, you would have dide to see Pewt spit and holler and drink water. he drank most of a gallon and he wont speak to me becaus i laffed.

All the Chadwicks got birned when they were blowing up old Buzell's fence posts, they was lots of fites down town and a house on

111

Franklin Street and a barn on Stratam Road birned up. it was the best 4th i ever gnew. Father sed about 2 more 4ths and he wood go out of bisiness.

i sed 2 4ths is eigt and he sed dont you try to be funny. if you do you will get a bat in the ear. so i shet up. when father says that it is about time to shet up.

"Tommy burned his fingers, Teddy burned his thumb,
Bobby burst the head of his brand-new drum,
Danny scorched his trousers, Dicky hurt his eye,
But we all had a GLORIOUS Fourth of July!"

—Harriet Brewer Sterling

★

AMERICA

BY
SAMUEL FRANCIS SMITH

My country, 'tis of thee,
Sweet land of liberty,
    Of thee I sing;
Land where my fathers died,
Land of the pilgrims' pride,
From every mountain-side
    Let freedom ring.

My native country, thee,
Land of the noble free,—
    Thy name I love;
I love thy rocks and rills,
Thy woods and templed hills;
My heart with rapture thrills
    Like that above.

Let music swell the breeze,
And ring from all the trees;
  Sweet freedom's song;
Let mortal tongues awake,
Let all that breathe partake,
Let rocks their silence break,—
  The sound prolong.

Our fathers' God, to thee,
Author of liberty,
  To thee I sing;
Long may our land be bright
With freedom's holy light;
Protect us by thy might,
  Great God our King.

THE BIG BASH OF 1919

In 1919, the foreign governments with which the United States had allied during World War I arranged for a special July 4th celebration in Washington, D.C., as a unique expression of their appreciation.

Festivities began at five P.M. with a series of tableaux representing "Bugle Call to World Service," "Call of Labor," "Call of Children," "Call of Art," "Call of the Land," and "Offering of Peace."

Then followed a parade of glorious floats down Pennsylvania Avenue, each nation's entry uniquely themed: **Haiti,** with a palm tree surrounded by a liberty cap; **Denmark,** with a Viking ship manned by a Viking and a figure of Peace; **China,** with a pavilion of peace surmounted by a golden phoenix; **Panama,** with a miniature canal entitled "Kiss of the Oceans"; **Guatemala,** with the temple of Minerva and a modern locomotive (for this was the first Central American country to build a transcontinental railroad); **Norway,** with a Viking ship with Leif Eriksson in command; **Peru,** with a series of tableaux showing life in that country; **Great Britain,** with a figure of Britannia seated on a throne behind a miniature garden featuring a maypole surrounded by dancing children; **Persia,** with Omar Khayyám seated among Persian rugs; **Greece,** with the Parthenon and Athena surrounded by maidens posed with urns on their shoulders; **Belgium,** with seven young women, mounted, and carrying flags; **Japan,** with figures representing Peace and Independence, seated upon a miniature Fujiyama; **France,** with a figure representing the Spirit of Advancement, on an elevated dais over two figures representing Alsace and Lorraine, joined to the upper figure by wreaths of laurel; **Italy,** with a reproduction of *Il Carrochia*, or "The Chariot," representing the victorious battle of Legano in 1176; and **Chile,** with five young women representing the country's five chief products.

> "There can be no fifty-fifty Americanism
> in this country. There is room here for only
> one-hundred-percent Americanism, only for those
> who are Americans and nothing else."
>
> —*Theodore Roosevelt, July 1918*

★

ON THIS DAY IN HISTORY, JULY 4TH

1924, Caesar Cardini of Tijuana, Mexico, is busily inventing the Caesar Salad. Running short of food as more customers than he expects descend on his popular restaurant, and thinking he can divert the crowd with a show, Cardini wheels a cart into the dining room and begins to make a salad with the ingredients at hand: romaine leaves, garlic-steeped olive oil, sprinkled salt (gentle tossing), eggs coddled for precisely one minute, lemon juice, Worcestershire sauce (toss the salad again), a showing of grated Parmesan, and croutons baked in garlic oil. *Voilà!* (There were no anchovies except for those in the Worcestershire sauce—the original Caesar was subtle.)

1935, for just five dollars, kids are ordering the "Children's Assortment" from the American Fireworks Distributing Company; included are four boxes of sparklers, twelve Python Black Snakes, twelve pounds of various-sized firecrackers, a Catherine wheel, firepots, and Roman candles—a total of fifty-six really dangerous things!

1939, Lou Gehrig retires at Yankee Stadium in front of seventy thousand heartbroken fans.

1944, General Omar Bradley, in celebration of July 4th, has every single artillery piece along the entire European front fixed on a target . . . and then he orders them fired at precisely noon. *Blam!!!*

1945, Vicksburg, Mississippi, celebrates July 4th for the first time in over eighty years, so angry have Vicksburgers been about what happened in 1863. The healing powers of World War II patriotism have finally won them over.

Philadelphia in 1951, upon the 175th anniversary of the Declaration of Independence, oak seedlings—planted in soil brought in from Revolutionary battlegrounds and mixed with that of the city's Independence Square—are sent to the governors of all forty-eight states as "symbols of new life springing from earth consecrated by the patriots of 1776."

1954, in Addis Ababa, Ethiopia, hundreds of Americans sing national songs, enjoy fireworks, and eat lots of hot dogs.

1959, when the forty-nine-star flag—for the new state of Alaska and the first change in the nation's ensign since 1912—is first raised, there are so many requests for flags flown over the Capitol on this day, that from midnight, through the dawn's early light, eight arm-weary Capitol guards raise and lower 1,072 new 49-star flags.

1960, not only is the fiftieth star added to the American flag as a symbol of Hawaii's statehood, but in the Battersea Pleasure Garden of London, eighty thousand American servicemen and their families enjoy the Fourth of July with a picnic of hot dogs and doughnuts and a day-long beauty contest.

1970, the "silent majority" turns out for a massive Honor America Day celebration at the Lincoln Memorial in Washington, D.C., featuring the Reverend Billy Graham and lots of police to keep out liberal freaks who have also come to town, for their own marijuana "smoke-in" and reflecting pool "wade-in."

The War (The Big One!) Years

On July 4, 1941, Emperor Hirohito kindly cabled Independence Day greetings to President Roosevelt. Then, five months later, he bombed the hell out of Pearl Harbor.

The nation absolutely devoted its resources to the war effort. Gas, silk (for parachutes), and food were rationed. The only wartime Independence Day celebrations were those at military bases, where July 4th was chosen for ceremonies to honor those killed in action.

In 1943, July 4th fell on a Sunday. In years past, to honor the Sabbath, holiday celebrations had traditionally been delayed twenty-four hours and Monday, July 5, became the official holiday. But in 1943, the war efforts were so pressing that factories could not close for even a day. The holiday was, essentially, skipped.

Those factories of the explosives and gunpowder industries were especially pressed into production. Of course, this meant no fireworks or firecrackers at all. So that in the end, what concerned parents, reformers, endless editorials, state laws, and local laws could never do, the war absolutely did—for the first time in nearly 180 years, July 4th was quiet.

In the postwar years, much of the population shifted to the suburbs, to developments without the deep-rooted traditions of more established communities. For many, a proper celebration was elusive; or that is, until the first person put a barbecue and a keg of beer in his suburban backyard and invited over friends and family. *Voilà!* A new and different Fourth of July! A tradition is born! Hamburgers, hot dogs, watermelon, potato salad, volleyball, horseshoes, and maybe a drive (in the suburban station wagon!) to the beach or over to the local park or high school for evening fireworks.

So, at the beginning of the country's third one hundred years, most Americans now celebrate their nation's birthday in a more private fashion, enjoying a summer afternoon with food and friends while not so many remain true to the traditional community-based affair.

FLAGGING YOUR BOAT

July 4th is the day on which you can finally unearth those forty or so signal flags (that someone—just who was it?—gave you for a birthday present) from the "flag locker" (under the AC cable below the port V-berth) and use them to glorify the nation's birthday. Dress ship!—an arcane but lovely vestige of naval glory that is now, unfortunately, more often seen at a yacht broker's open house than in the local harbor.

According to Chapman's *Piloting, Seamanship and Small Boat Handling,* "A rainbow of flags of the International Code is arranged reaching from the waterline aft by way of the bowsprit end or stem (if there is no bowsprit) and the masthead(s). Flags (letters) and pennants (numerals) are bent on alternately rather than in any indiscriminate manner. Since there are more letters than numerals . . . it is a good practice . . . to follow a sequence of two flags, one pennant, two flags, one pennant throughout."

You can also fly the U.S. national ensign or the U.S. yacht ensign on the stern staff and the Union Jack at the bow or jack staff.

This dressing can be flown from 0900 until evening colors. Ahoy, mates!

Concord Hymn
by
Ralph Waldo Emerson

By the rude bridge that arched the flood,
Their flag to April's breeze unfurled,
Here once the embattled farmers stood,
And fired the shot heard round the world.

The foe long since in silence slept;
Alike the conqueror silent sleeps;
And Time the ruined bridge has swept
Down the darkstream which seaward creeps.

On this green bank, by this soft stream,
We set to-day a votive stone;
That memory may their deed redeem,
When, like our sires, our sons are gone.

Spirit, that made those heroes dare
To die, and leave their children free,
Bid Time and Nature gently spare
the shaft we raise to them and thee.

THE BICENTENNIAL BASH
July 4, 1976 — The 200th Birthday!

The Continental Congress by resolution adopted July 2, 1776, declared that thirteen American colonies were free and independent states. Two days later, on the fourth of July, the Congress adopted a Declaration of Independence which proclaimed to the world the birth of the United States of America.

In the two centuries that have passed, we have matured as a nation and as a people. We have gained the wisdom that age and experience bring, yet we have kept the strength and idealism of youth.

In this year of our nation's Bicentennial, we enter our third century with the knowledge that we have achieved greatness as a nation and have contributed to the good of mankind. We face the future with renewed dedication to the principles embodied in our Declaration of Independence, and with renewed gratitude for those who pledged their lives, their fortunes and their sacred honor to preserve individual liberty for us.

In recognition of the two-hundredth anniversary of the great historic events of 1776, and in keeping with the wishes of the Congress, I ask that all Americans join in an extended period of celebration, thanksgiving, and prayer on the second, third, fourth, and fifth days of July of our bicentennial year—so that people of all faiths in their own way may give thanks for the protection of Divine Providence through two hundred years, and pray for the future safety and happiness of our nation.

To commemorate the adoption of the Declaration of Independence, the Congress, by concurrent resolution adopted June 26, 1963 (77 Stat. 944), declared that its anniversary be observed by the ringing of bells throughout the United States.

NOW, THEREFORE, I, Gerald R. Ford, President of the United States of America, do hereby proclaim that the two hundredth anniversary of the adoption of the Declaration of Independence be observed by the simultaneous ringing of bells throughout the United States at the hour of two o'clock, Eastern Daylight Time, on the afternoon of the Fourth of July, 1976, our Bicentennial Independence Day, for a period of two minutes, signifying our two centuries of independence.

I call upon civic, religious, and other community leaders to encourage public participation in this historic observance, I call upon all Americans, here and abroad, including all United States flagships at sea, to join in our salute.

As the bells ring in our third century, as millions of free men and women pray, let every American resolve that this nation, under God, will meet the future with the same courage and dedication Americans showed the world two centuries ago. In perpetuation of the joyous ringing of the Liberty Bell in Philadelphia, let us again "proclaim liberty throughout all the land unto all the inhabitants thereof."

IN WITNESS WHEREOF, I have here unto set my hand this twenty-ninth day of June in the year of our Lord nineteen hundred seventy-six, and of the Independence of the United States of America the two hundredth.

—Gerald R. Ford

"I shall know but one country. The ends I aim
at shall be my country's, my God's, and Truth's. I was
born an American; I will live an American; I shall
die an American."

—Daniel Webster, July 1850

The Bicentennial Administration, headed by former Navy secretary John Warner, determined that the Bicentennial would be composed of hundreds of small-scale, local celebrations, with the Administration acting only as a kind of clearinghouse to list the multitude of diverse events. Seemingly anything and everything—"All you have to do is apply!"—could be included on the official list of Bicentennial events.

Sunrise on the nation's two hundredth birthday came first to the tiny, potato-growing town of Mars Hill, Maine, where National Guardsmen fired a fifty-gun salute and raised the American Flag. Then a multitude of other events unfolded, including

- the erection of a giant goose statue in Summer, Montana—"Wild Goose Capital of the World";
- the serving of a spaghetti dinner for three thousand—including six hundred pounds of pasta and six hundred pounds of sausage—in Rome, New York;
- a shuffleboard contest in Truth or Consequences, New Mexico;
- the naturalization of *1,776* new citizens at Chicago Stadium;

- the planting of a young buttonwood Liberty Tree in Newport, Rhode Island, next to the very tree planted at the Centennial, on the exact spot where the British troops chopped down the town's original Liberty Tree;
- a Bicentennial Buffalo Supper in Gary, South Dakota;
- the lofting of the largest national flag ever—193 feet by 366-1/2 feet, bigger by half than a football field, costing $45,000 and weighing 1-1/2 tons—from the Verrazano-Narrows Bridge at the entrance to New York harbor, to welcome the Tall Ships;
- the crossing of Miami's Biscayne Bay by George Washington, standing tall in a handsome uniform, his booted foot resting on the seat of a motorboat;
- the full-dress reenactment of a Revolutionary battle at Flushing Meadows Park in Queens, New York, where no fighting actually took place during the Revolution;
- a beard-judging contest in Bristol, Rhode Island;
- a Boston Bicentennial Concert featuring pop singer Elton John dressed as the Statue of Liberty in a silver-sequined robe;
- a chili championship in San Marcos, Texas;

130

- a Bicentennial Parade in Bartow, Florida, featuring honorary grand marshal Charlie Smith, who is also celebrating his 134th birthday and who arrived in New Orleans on a slave ship in 1854 (he is the only one in town who remembers the Centennial);
- a parade of 212 sailing ships from thirty-four nations sailing up the Hudson River in New York City under the view of millions, including President Ford who, at 2 P.M., aboard the aircraft carrier U.S.S. *Forrestal,* rang the ship's bell thirteen times in honor of the original thirteen colonies; and,
- at the same time, in Philadelphia, descendants of those who signed the Declaration of Independence gently tapping on the Liberty Bell with a rubber mallet.

That evening, in Washington, D.C., over two million people watched thirty-three tons of fireworks explode in a fabulous display over the Washington Monument. The display, which cost $200,000, was put together by Etablissements Ruggieri, the same French firm that concocted a display seen by Thomas Jefferson in Paris in 1786.

BICENTENNIAL TRIVIA

In 1976, ten different parties climbed Mount McKinley—the tallest peak in North America—and reached its peak on July 4, causing between eight hundred and a thousand people to be on top the crowded mountain at the same time.

The celebration of the Tall Ships in New York City, the most spectacular of all the Bicentennial festivities in 1976, was to include 226 sailing ships from 31 nations, but that was reduced to 225 ships from 30 nations when at least six kilos of cocaine were discovered aboard Colombia's entry, *Gloria.*

The official Bicentennial parade in the nation's capital was led by Vice President Nelson Rockefeller, his wife, Happy, and Johnny Cash.

New York harbor's huge Bicentennial fireworks display demanded the transportation of fireworks from as far away as Orlando, Florida, the digging of sixty-foot trenches on Ellis Island, bringing three barges in from Poughkeepsie, installing an automated control point in the World Trade Center, setting up huge spotlights on

Liberty Island and heavy racks on Governor's Island, seventy-ton cranes to unload five hundred mortars to fire more than three thousand shells, two-and-a-half-ton searchlights, and more than two thousand light bulbs.

★

The Glory of Red, White, and Blue (RWB) in 1976

1. The wrecker trucks at the Indianapolis Speedway are now RWB.

2. At Philadelphia's Memorial Hall, the biggest birthday cake ever made—five stories high and 200,000 servings—is covered in RWB icing.

3. Alcatraz, that erstwhile bastion of non-liberty, is featuring RWB fireworks.

4. Boston's garbage trucks are now RWB.

5. The two 3-story radar domes at Alaska's remote (on top of the world) Campion Air Force Station are now painted with RWB stars and '76s.

6. The restaurant chain Waffle Houses is coloring its product RWB for the time being.

7. Over 2 million Americans graduating from high school are wearing a RWB cap tassel.

8. Illinois, Michigan, Indiana, the District of Columbia, South Carolina, Montana, and Hawaii now have RWB license plates (although Hawaii's red came out parlor-pink).

9. Cleveland's thirteen thousand fireplugs—all of them!—are RWB.

In the 1970s, the concept of running around (jogging) suddenly brought popular endorsement to one of the Fourth's quieter traditions—the marathon. The granddaddy of the many July 4th runs is the Mount Marathon Race, which begins in downtown Seward, Alaska, then ascends and descends 3,022-foot Mt. Marathon. This grueling competition first began over a quarter century ago as a wager between two sourdoughs. More recent entries in the marathon include the 10K Lenexa, Kansas, Freedom Run, the 10K Peachtree Road Race in Atlanta, the 17K Anvil Mountain Run outside Nome, Alaska, and the eight-mile Independence Day Challenge Run in Boyne City, Michigan.

1922 marks the first Annual Greeley Spud Rodeo and Fourth of July Celebration in Greeley, Colorado. The big day features rodeo contests like bucking horses, steer roping, and cow milking.

The Great Depression of the early 1930s put a nearly permanent damper in the nation's celebration of its Independence Day. With the severely reduced budgets of all municipalities, little or no money was spent on bunting, parades, costumes, and fireworks. For example, on July 4, 1937, the top July 4th events in New York City included festivities by the Communist Party, the Italian Anti-Fascist Committee, and the annual flag-raising at City Hill Park by the elderly United American Spanish War Veterans.

On July 4, 1946, speeches, flag raisings, circling planes, parades, and a twenty-one-gun salute mark the official independence of the Philippines. The big occasion, first scheduled for 1944, was delayed by two years because of World War II.

Throughout the 1950s, Americans hesitate in their celebration of the Fourth. The traditions of a hundred years no longer neatly fit these unfamiliar times—Americans are dying, as if at war, in a Korean "police action"; schoolchildren rehearse weekly for that frightening split second when the A-bomb will drop into their neighborhood; and invisible communist anarchists are believed to be running amok throughout the nation's once-trusted governments, from

Congress to the local recreation-and-parks committee. Many communities calm their July 4th celebrations, lessening the noise and activities, and turn to the re-dedication of proven shrines and battlefields. Quiet ceremonies are most often held at tried-and-true locations like Valley Forge, the Washington Monument, Philadelphia's Independence Hall, and the Old State House in Boston.

In 1958, more than 200,000 persons jammed the shores of the Potomac River in Washington to celebrate the Fourth by dedicating Theodore Roosevelt Island. Maryland's Governor Theodore Roosevelt McKeldin concluded his dedication address noting that this wildlife preserve was now a site for "peace and quiet." Then the loudest fireworks display ever, up to that time in the nation's history, was let loose.

In 1959, the citizens of Scarsdale, New York, were awarded the George Washington Medal of Honor by the Freedom Foundation for having given the funds allocated for fireworks to the American Korean Foundation. Thousands of Scarsdalians then complemented their philanthropic efforts with a July 4th featuring Korean music and dancing.

Those same Scarsdalians, in 1960, held a festive July 4th that focused attention on Morocco, which had "suffered tragically from the use of adulterated cooking oil."

AROUND THE WORLD IN '76

In celebration of the American Bicentennial . . .

Middlesbrough, England mounts a show of American gravestone rubbings;

Hay-on-Wye, Wales sponsors a book sale, which features American books published in 1776, 1876, and 1976;

West Germany hosts four thousand different American bicentennial projects; Belgium, 45; Monaco, 20;

Great Britain gives the United States a gold replica of the Magna Carta;

Edinburgh, Scotland, features Princess Grace of Monaco, back on stage, reciting American poetry;

Israel creates a thousand-acre Bicentennial Park;

Singapore mounts a twenty-six-inch-high Revere Bell;

Düsseldorf, Germany, sponsors rodeos;

Berlin features rock concerts;

The Soviets publish editions of works by modern American authors like Truman Capote;

France offers so many formal festivities that the U.S. embassy in Paris loses count.

THIS DAY IN HISTORY, ON JULY 4TH...

1982, as part of some diabolical right-wing campaign, thousands of crazed fundamentalists call the Phil Donahue and Merv Griffin TV shows to expose Procter and Gamble as a devil-worshipping firm because of its quarter-moon-and-stars logo.

1986, hundreds of Elvis Presley imitators perform in an official, sanctioned celebration of the nation's unveiling of the refurbished Statue of Liberty.

1994, just after Michael DeVito, a thirty-two-year-old accountant, wins the annual Coney Island Hot Dog–Eating Contest with the consumption of twenty hot dogs (his fourth victory in five years!), he notes, "I feel very full right now." Curtis Sliwa, the notorious leader of the Guardian Angels, who downs thirteen dogs, promises to "smoke" Mr. DeVito next year. "I learned a trick of the trade," he says. "DeVito squeezes the buns to make them smaller."

The United States Forest Service . . .

. . . has an annual Fourth of July tradition: It copes with "The Rainbow Family of Living Light," an annual gathering on public lands of nearly twenty thousand people who pray for world peace.

The Forest Service classifies the gathering as a "Type 1" incident. Oil spills and major forest fires also belong to the "Type 1" category. Within the Forest Service's official guidelines to its regional managers are the following recommendations and observations:

> Nudity is common, expect thousands of dogs—and some cats, birds, lizards, and llamas, begin, early on, to pressure the participants to dig the required number of latrines, almost any activity that does not hurt anyone is acceptable, and the event will dominate your life for two to three months; but it will go away.

★

"Let the annual return of this day
forever refresh our recollections of these rights,
and an undiminished devotion to them."

—*Thomas Jefferson*

FAMOUS LAST WORDS

"Is it the Fourth?"

> —*Thomas Jefferson, his last words, just prior to slipping into a coma, on July 3, 1826, concerned that he might die before the fiftieth anniversary of the Declaration of Independence*

"Thomas Jefferson still survives."

> —*John Adams, his last words, on July 4, 1826, the fiftieth anniversary of the Declaration of Independence. (Adams was wrong. Jefferson had died a few hours earlier, also on the Fourth.)*

147

Illustration and Photo Credits